First printing, 2020.

For **A**frica, the native land.

For **B**lack, the color that I am.

For **C**ommunity, a place of our own.

For **D**addy, a Black man strong.

For the Effort that he gives.

For the **F**amily where I live.

For **G**od, Almighty!

H

For **H**appy as I can be.

I can do anything.

For **J**oy, that makes me want to sing.

For **K**wanzaa we celebrate.

For **L**ove and no hate.

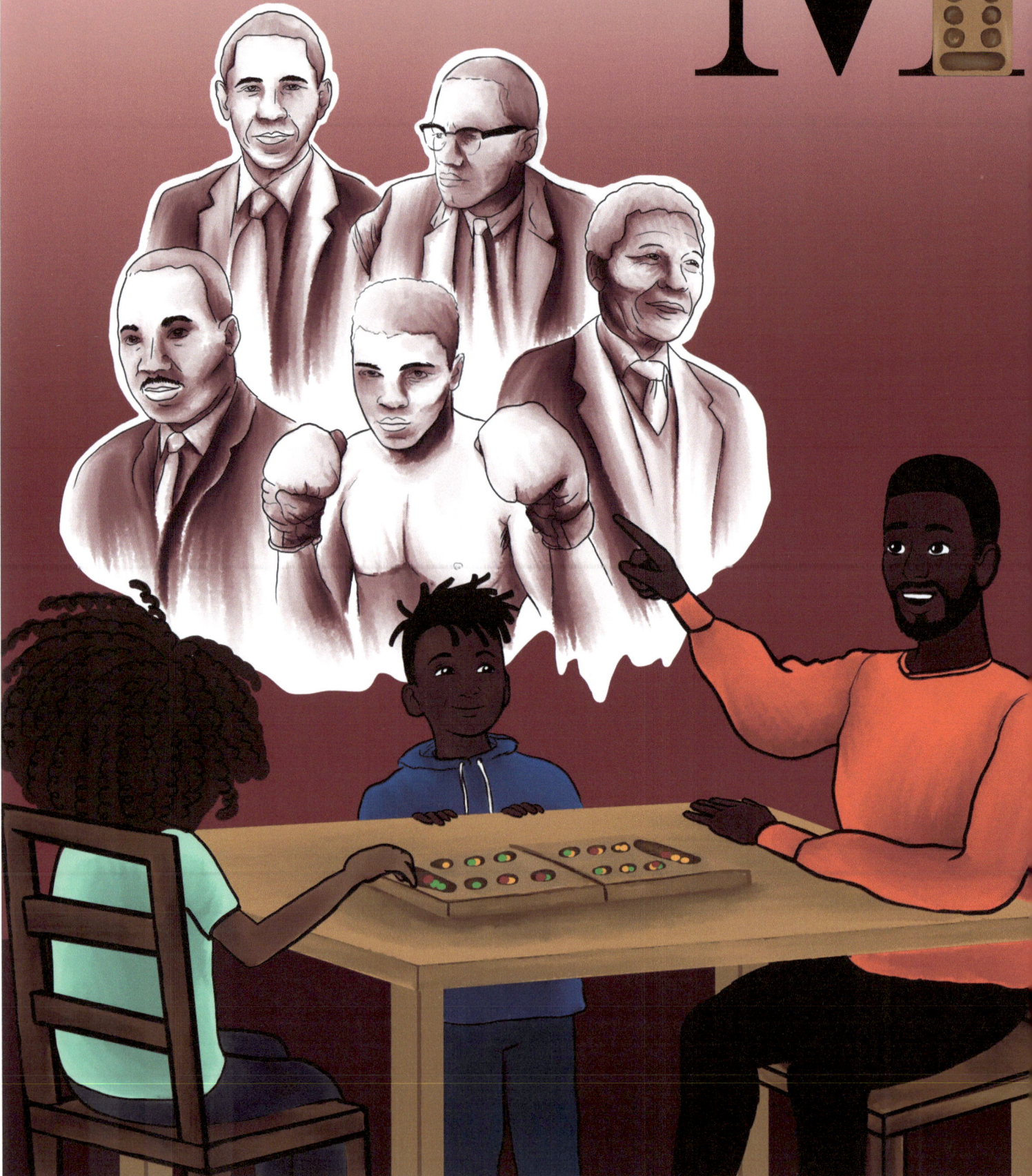

For **M**en helping us soar to new heights.

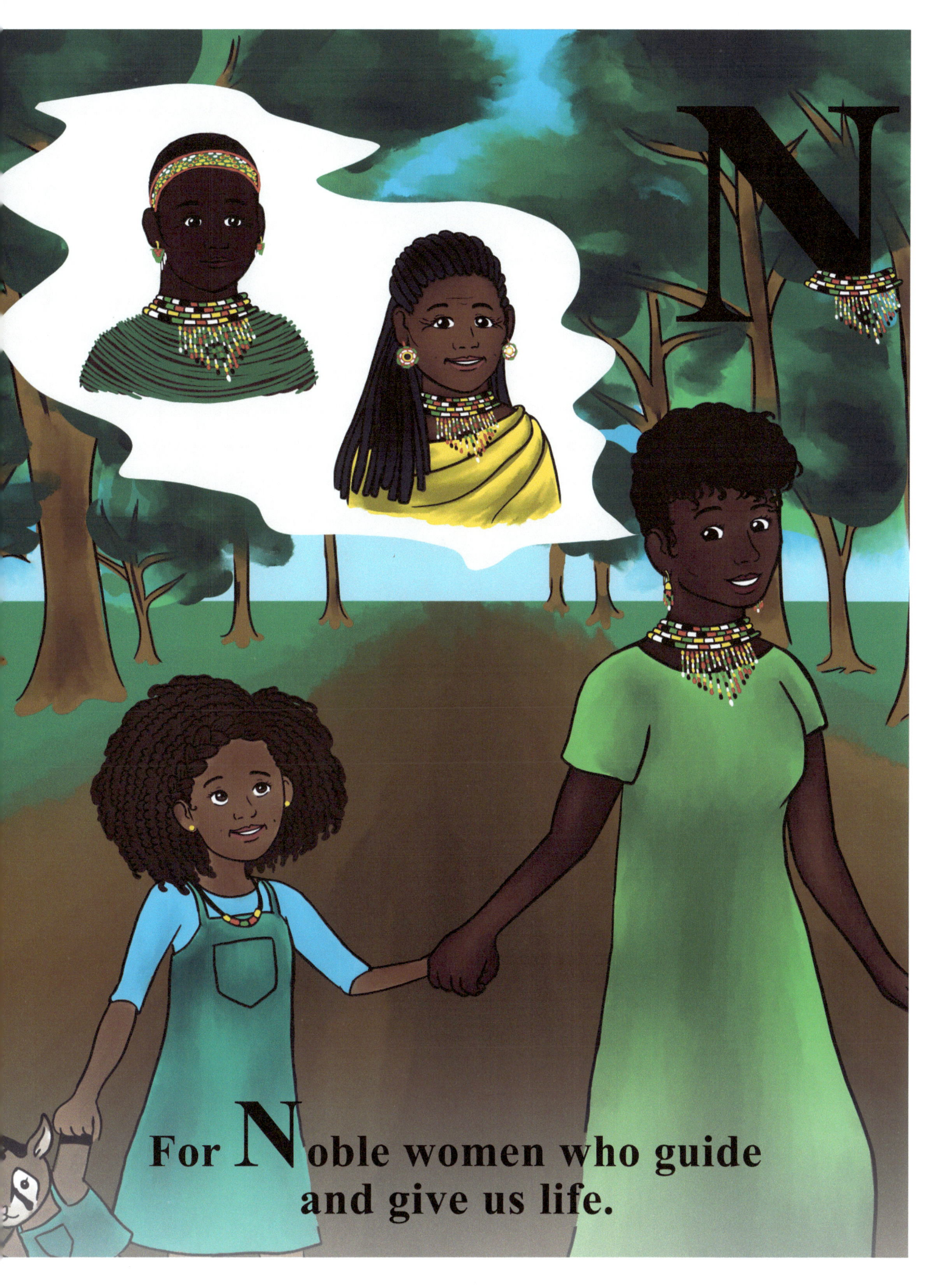

For **N**oble women who guide
and give us life.

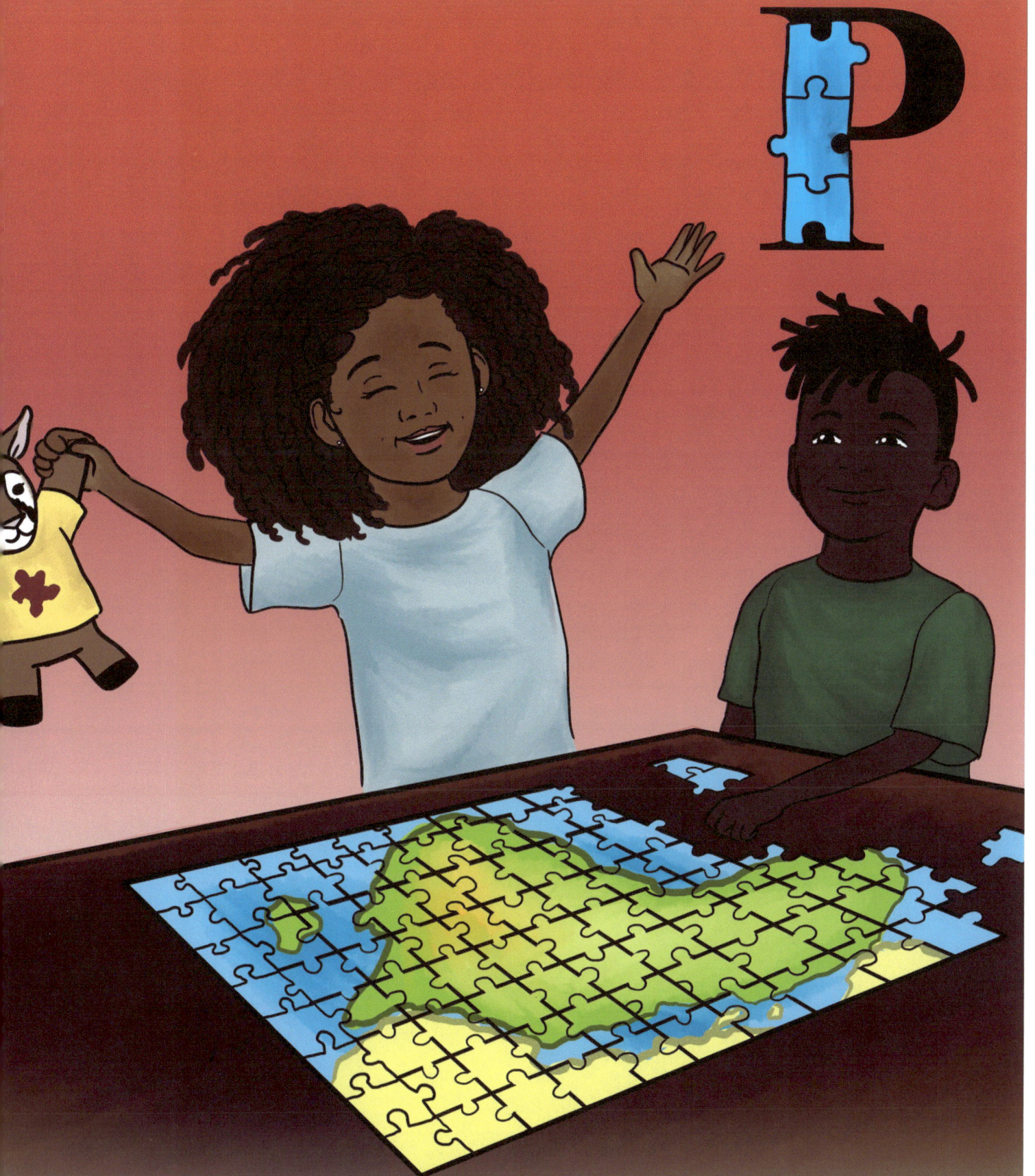

P

For being **P**roud. I want to stand up and yell!

For the Queens we appreciate.

Nefertiti
c. 1370-1330 BC

QUIZ

R

For Rap, Rhythm and Blues and Reggae.

For the **S**un shining on my face.

Today I start a brand-new race.

For **U**nity to get us ahead.

For Visions of my future
dancing in my head.

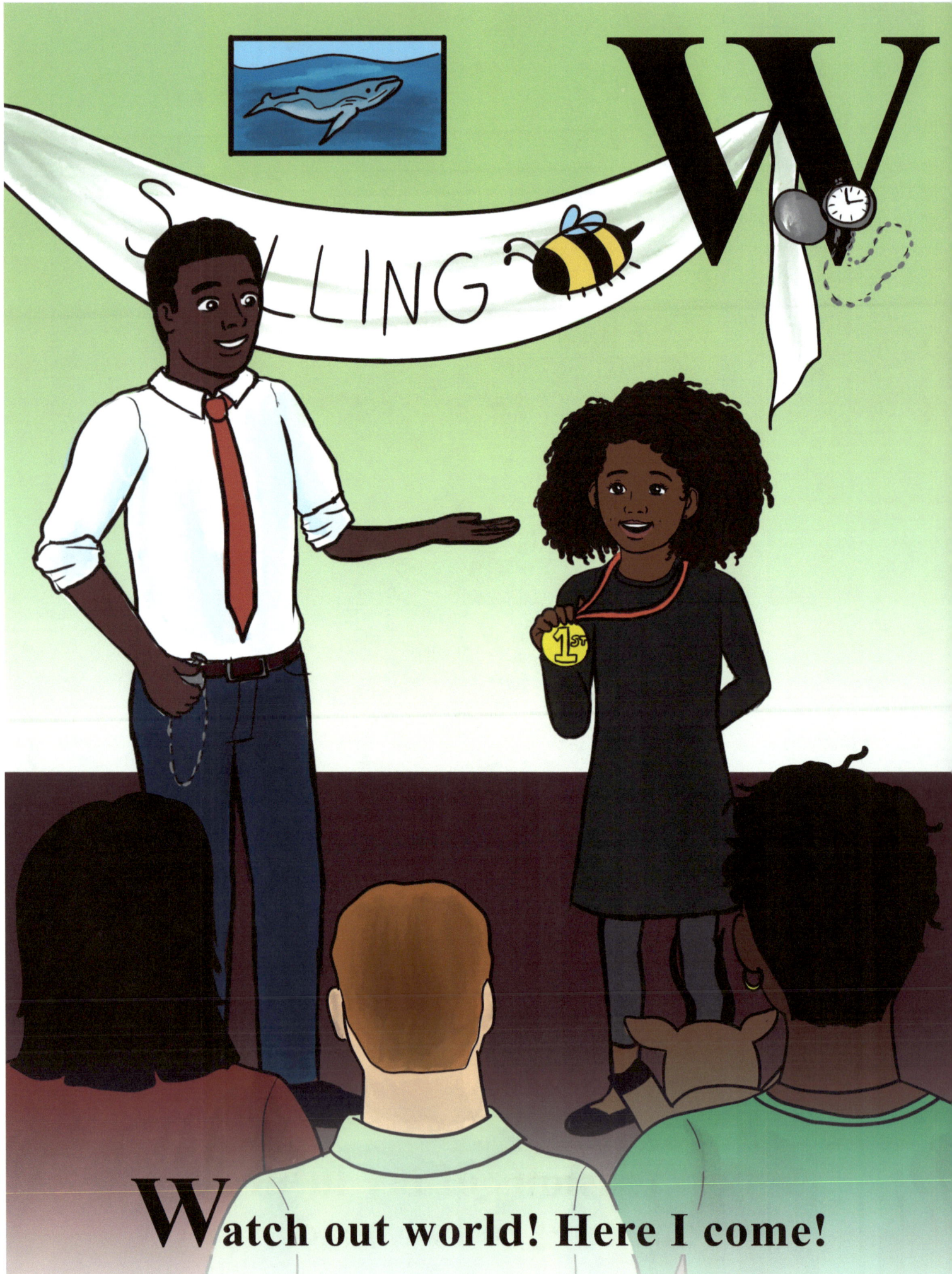

Watch out world! Here I come!

Xtra! Xcited! Wait! What about some food for my tummy, tum, tum?

For **Y**ummy, yummy, yams.
They're the best!

Y

For **Z**ip, zap, zoom! I'm full of zest. I'm ready to pass the AlphaBlack test!

About the Illustrator

Renee Miche'al Jones is a cultural educator/artist in the city of Dallas. For over two decades, she has performed and collaborated educational arts programs with local and regional educators to provide diversity awareness in the public-school arena. She holds a Bachelor of Science in Human Ecology from the University of Texas at Austin and is currently pursuing a Master of Science in Child and Adolescent Development Psychology from Northcentral University in San Diego, California. AlphaBlack is the first children's book in her repertoire of products.

As part of her endeavor to teach cultural awareness to urban youth, she founded Roots for Youth. RFY is a cognitive learning system aimed at providing cultural relevance and knowledge of the African diaspora. Through RFY, she has presented storytelling, workshops and residencies to community organizations such as the City of Dallas Office of Cultural Affairs, Pan African Connection Bookstore and Resource Center, The Esudele Fagbenro Institute of Arts & Culture, Big Thought, and Junior Players. She continues her quest to provide essential African cultural resources to educators by completing additional children's books, theatrical performances, and cognitive learning games.

About the Illustrator

Kelsey Hoff is a designer and illustrator with a deep love for visual storytelling. She holds a Bachelor of Science in Virtual Technology and Design with a minor in Fine Art. By day she works as a Digital Illustrator in the tech industry and moonlights as an illustrator and layout designer for print and digital books. AlphaBlack is the fifth book she has designed for but is her very first illustrated children's book.